CARNAVORIA

Laurie Saurborn Young

H_NGM_N BKS
www.h-ngm-nbks.com

FIRST H_NGM_N EDITION, 2012

Copyright © 2012 by Laurie Saurborn Young

ISBN 978-0-9832215-6-2

Cover photograph by Liubomir Turcanu
Cover design by Scott O'Connor
Book design by Nate Slawson

for Dean

Even a wrong course one sometimes ought to pursue
to its end, till refusal of praise becomes praise.

–H. L. Hix

CONTENTS

CARNAVORIA

The Name of the World

Five swimmers, a dark lake, and the moon.
Oh, night knows nothing of green grass.

And day knows little of silhouette. We are
wading out and slipping off in bodies, how-

ever incomplete. Existing for a deep while,
embraced. Our plans for the stars will cease.

Bottles grow warm on the dock.
Our world rings, the shape we make as

we present the fact of our bodies to water.

*

As though it is difficult to claim a love
in this world where everyone is half

misunderstood. Petals in ink; the dog
watches from the bank. We are here, we

are not. We come and divide, as animals
do. Cicadas in the trees, their raspy sex

calls us back. A few of us swim farther
as the lake and the moon think over this

single fact of our floating between them.

*

Rest here, the swimmer says to the body.
We must stop counting the ways we

have not yet become who we were.
A fraction of turtle, a sliver of royalty:

we are more than the fight of our history.
More than the lover taken into water.

9

We depart as possibility, rings run through.
The name of the world is inconstant

and there is a young blue star behind us.

Chevalier of the Air

How dark was our one evening by the shore?
    Dim enough to blend a shirt into phosphorescence;

        light enough for you to see the back of my head.
            Now I'm just a woman who throws her dress

        on the floor, who tries to convert hydrogen into gold.
    I wish I could tell you it's easier now, but I suspect

love can wear out. My sister keeps the museum: damp
    flames of morning swims, of rainy afternoons

        stretched over musty carpet. Oh how we become
            a tally of hallucination and memory, unreleased—

        daffodils in our teeth for one dance, tiger in our laps
    over a winter evening. My body Rome, I leave as I burn:

each day a little more red coal, a bit more ash as
    I gather myself into a net and hook onto the basket

        of a passing balloon. A war-loved blanket, wool
            mittens, an oar to paddle the air—what my sister

        throws to me. How light it is here. How I confessed,
    lakeside, to never reading a lover's diary. I promise

to wave from high altitudes, these heights where I recall
    faith was easier when love appeared on time. No way to predict

        how we'll waste our efforts. How light it is where I imagine
    your glow, as I trace the stubborn back of my own head.

A woman drinks a morning glass of wine under an over-
    cast sky. Maybe she is writing a letter to those

        friends who have moved on and to the way currents
            taste when the sun is in the east and beloved.

Wife of Bird

Afternoons I dress as a metal owl.
I strive to recognize the importance
of wide flight among narrow pines.

A man behind the counter peeks
over at me. My eyes are two barrels.

How the man brings the coffee says
Summer's a dead time here, bird.
A bite to his thigh and I run out,

miner's hat in hand, canaries in my ears.
I do not know what to do,
                                        so I grow older.

So I make satin coats for all the doves.
Only April and the ground is cracking.
I pour cups of water into the air

to wash the young dragonflies.

Four

Swimming in the pool, skin still
tight over muscle, I saw your slow

plow through the lane. Lips only blue
from the cold. I couldn't keep pace,

my breath a mis-matched step.
A year later and you are looking up

from your hospital bed, asking
How did you alight me here?

I stroke your hand until flight is all
we remember. Stone doors opening,

closing in my chest. People
are no good at dying but they

keep on with it anyway.
I put my head down on the bars

and wake when the doctor comes in.

Moving Costs

For these years we are brave and we march along the farm, singing dirt.
A tiny town in California is no place to leave my sister and so I stayed.

Asymmetric haircuts, our heads connect as the clouds give way.
Gorgeous, we watch our skin marching to our fingertips.

We stand with hands above our heads and cannot pretend grass.
No place for my sister, this town, but here she found her dog and stayed.

So stay the bricks in the chimney; so stays the groundhog in the trap.
We cover potatoes in red bright dresses. We envy the swish of their skirts.

Remaining in one field won't slow the rise and decline of raspberries,
tatters in the knees and seat. I count coyotes from the porch. For bears,

my sister illustrates the dangers of coveting garbage. Of course, of course
bears never listen and coyotes sip drinks, lick straws like the blowjobs

they mostly hate to give. So much to suffer through, just to say you've won.
Mornings, the neighbor shoots a groundhog so we refuse to share

his haircut. We take dresses from the potatoes then ask the berries *Just
how things are* this summer. My sister and I run through corn and core;

my sister is several symphonies she cannot hear. Furniture we've bought
and abandoned could fill the house we don't yet know and cannot pretend.

For these years, the dirt sings. For these years we try on brave and breathe.
Thirsty, we create a still from the potatoes that little know their potential,

having given up on bears and coyotes. We invite a man who does the washing,
who doesn't believe in wandering clouds. Cups of clarity, my sister in a red

hat. I weave a scarf through my fingers and tie an apron on the man.
He brings us piles of pale folded flowers and we are enough in the farm.

Our hands at our sides we watch the clouds leaning away, no suffering.
At night coyotes call from the field, their cries coils of escaping heat.

The bear tries to dissuade the groundhog from traps and over the course of five days the man reappears to disappear, departure as this world.

I twist myself up in flowers folded or in the pale calls of animals moving past. My sister tires of the corn; she throws apples for her dog to catch.

We stay and wait to hear back from bravery as it burrows toward the sea.

That Neighbor

In the city, a dog's footsteps on the sidewalk
leave inverse shadows. Babies sing as spoons

clatter in far-off mouths and wide jars.
I string imaginary trip wires in the front yard

but no one ever walks toward the house.
A pile of snakes is such a plain thing to fear.

I should draw my hair up in a tangled manner
and eat cabbage for breakfast each morning.

People I don't know are crying and I am glad
it is not me, the unknown person, crying.

Dogs sing as babies sleep in convex shadows.
I knock on doors. I hand over cake and pliers.

Confession Twenty-Seven

So it is true: I am all types of scenery.
A translucent multiple of unmastered
views. Every panel has its own certain

rhyme, its slow days in slow graze. All
clothes belie the frame outside. It will
come to no matter what slips to the floor

when a woman and a man hear this fact:
a bird's tongue curls around its brain.
There, the similarities end. Small wonder,

glass-grain shore: the lake is slowly seeking
further forms. Again the knowledge
of knowing what needs to be done, walking

toward me like a goose. Casting around
for anything quick to toss to the buoy.
My will is a sugar cube held in the teeth.

The sun praises in rotation. Hours are left
out in the elements until it is clear my
cards will not return to claim me. I confess

I desire the clean spill of milk over tables,
the whole hand in one pocket. It is fine
to be tired at dawn and again at noon. Glitter

clings to skin as I stop to watch a beetle
rest in sanded shadows. It does not matter
where I am. Here is the best inch in view.

Life as an Uncast Spell

Magic hat, upend the rabbits. Somersault past the saw.
Someone turns and the stage is getting darker on itself.
Crackers for accident, crackers for the dumb bird.
Throw it all on the floor. We will dance like meteors.
In the aisles we step on everyone's feet.
You can't breathe on the way to the store
And it feels like kissing!
Like staring at women as a way to see myself.
I make a little bird to tell everyone but it dies or is lost.
Gracious catastrophe, so gentle on the ear—
For years I waited to turn into someone else,
Into a collection of looks from across the room.
What can I predict for our photons scrambling out?
We know so little of what sits above our necks.
The breath, spilling up from below, says
Time's up, it has been years so move into the new verdant.
Meanwhile, I didn't like anyone, stars cluttering up the day.
And now the floor is burning until it is atmosphere.
I don't know if it is possible, but I'm wearing a dress all the same.
Tap a dove three times on the beak and its feathers fall out.
And it becomes a fable, a tiger with velvet eyes.

Upon the Court Jester's Eviction

To where are you heading off, funny man,
with your arms covered in tears? To where

are you walking, all laugh and hands? Once
we kissed and it kept me clear for years.

Last night you paneled the court in rusted
tin. You marked the perimeter with a wooden

spoon. The cooks crying, our empty king
humming to metal noise hanging in the air.

To where are you heading, no bells no tricks?
Dearest, in the next location of your arrival

I will continue to never spend the night.
But I will bring a sky and it will convince

you to look up, just as the ground compelled
me to go. In my hands I will hold melody,

the commotion of tin in air, the bodies of kings.
We will sit by a window watching time lie

asleep outside. My horsemen drinking to where
ever and me washing salt from your skin.

My Mother was an Anthropologist

Driving along the underside of the planet

we keep old bones in the truck bed,

waiting for something to call autumn amid

birds with their beaks open to the heat.

I spread butter against the bread's heart.

If you don't believe everything captures

a soul, then perhaps you too are caught

in the gravity of sleep and wake? It's

something like kissing lovers in dreams

but with a touch more salt and a new

ability to stop time—just long enough

to enjoy the experience of having earth

by the balls. Of driving backwards over

corn fields wherein you dropped many

mittens one winter while turning into

someone with a slightly taller shadow.

From the Deck of Periodic Flight

Does it matter who wipes water
from the sills after it has rained
all afternoon? Either way, time

passes on the body. We take pictures
of bridges so as to remember a
more intermediary gravity.

I would write the equation down
but all the tables are evaporating.
So I put on a hat and keep going.

What Can I Tell You

What can you tell me in passing, what can you say
about the screens drying in the sun? Once I had a niece
but I left her out in the sun too long. I left her with

> wedding china, old pictures of camping trips,
> a cat hiding under the bed. Each night I dream
> of what I left behind, though there is little of it

I still want: I want under the bed with the cat.
I want plates with green rabbits; a niece, watering
stumps. Someone I loved claimed I had a knack for setting

> a domestic scene, but they discounted a fire in the corner.
> No idea if I'll see you again, pieces of our bodies breaking
> off into wind. Three pecan trees died and I took

one down. Here, windows are never wide enough
to see who might float along this road. Girls with soft
cheekbones, with hair knotted. I have never kissed them

> and the house next door still rots. Little good but
> the boy, riding his bike until his mother takes it away.
> But the boy, talking to the neighbors until his mother takes

him away. The woman across the street, still dying
after two years. I had hoped we could be friends.
Not the woman and me, but you and I. You are gone,

> and I still don't know how the front walk came
> to be stained with mulberries when there are none
> for miles around. But mostly it is hard to sleep.

In many dreams I'm the stranger in a photograph,
the tiny woman just to the right of your shoulder.
I can tell you about moving ten times in four years;

> about the way most people think I fell from the sky.
> But I caught the wind, see. I caught on to the few
> branches with gravity to keep me upright and mostly

unreceptive to the girls I won't kiss. To the way
I will never see you again. Trucks drive by. Mulberries
ripen. There is a catalogue I keep with me, the list

      of everything I leave. I left my niece out in the sun
      and now she is fourteen. Of course my shy cat is dead.

Indirect Entry

On Tuesday someone gives me half a skeleton. It
fits into the lock and the door falls down, of course.
I step around the keyhole and everything becomes

clear. There are rooms of cars jumping cliffs; of girls
with hair in their eyes; of ships moving in the dark.
Faces look in to see what color the air is. To see

whether the beagle next door will rob us tonight.
Nine times out of ten is a recipe for bread. Is a voice
saying love is like tumbling through a trap door.

Air & Space

One is a child with blue mittens

telling me light tastes like cold rice.

Later, it's a woman with a bucket of water,
asking me to keep it safe in the lake.

Neither stay and as they each depart
they tell me I can always turn back.

                    Unafraid of children with snow

in their hair, of women and most bodies
of water, I say there is no place to stop. That

                there are stars we should step around.

To the woman I say, Tell me when
you strung snow on wires and it glowed

in the bedroom all spring.
There is ice on the brim of her hat;

a little falls off as she looks toward her feet.

Says I do not know if this matters—

                        I saw five finches today, but no sky.

Salvage Operation

When I say *wounded* I don't mean sadness.
I don't mean there was an accident.

I don't mean a deer in the New England fall,
or the look in your eyes when I threw your coat

out the car window one December night.
I mean that all day I say *I love you* until

I'm sure the schools and churches are tearing
my words from their fine and shining hair.

There are many planets we might end up on.
But here five horses dance into you all day.

Red dragonflies fly from the faucets. Roses
move in, and I no longer force myself upon

the arboretum. When I say *eyes* I mean
there are things I would rather not know.

Raised to be Assassins

We wash our cars with a feather and fresh rain.
         Our fingers are sticky in proof and we point

Upwards to what is afloat. The regular
         Appearance of departure in the way oaks

Catch the wind, branches bent for a bit of realism.
         The cards are so close they press into our eyes.

True, we are all combined in general dressings.
         We are prying up the floorboards to find the tape.

Remembering archers and their secrets, places
         To wash the car in the rain. How to lighten

The sky's edge with lemon. We leave inside one
         Ornament or we put our cups back into thin

Saucers. What is the brilliant admission? Our
         Breathing is corrected. We have one love over

Days and then suddenly remember seven.
         In the lesser carbons of our hearts, we shoot

Upwards, our cards so close they are all we see
         Awaiting. This brilliant realism caught and combined

Is the secret of an archer leaving a marker
         Behind. Casting out for a new subject until

All we can find are our hands, fluttering down.

To the Protractor's Muse

Let me in on your angle of approach.
Draw the wilted leaves up with string:
we are out of water and someone's

always bound to show. This house holds
islands, a few of them unsafe. Our eyes
will continue to weather all manner

of storm and what we thought we heard.
Never waste too much time on proof:
there is no power driving us to our

knees. I feel my way along by the bolts
in the floor, my desire the most vivid
black and white. Brief preparations

made for recognition's repetition,
how one meal brings to mind another.
This is where we are left, seeking pause

or praise. I can draw a flawless arc
if you'll just stay still. Listen while
grass breaks out in cat calls and trees

grow heavy in doves. Tonight, our
moon is null set. *Imagine my surprise
at my departure*, says our migratory world.

Young Love II

Oh, how secrets of heaven
string us along.

Every cell is a telescope.

Or every cell is nothing much
more than a kiss at noon.

I cup air in my hands.
Surf-deep we search for rocks

shot through with lightning.

*

For a silver line that trembles
when we touch.

What sand, what fumbling along

the strings. Flowers bloom in place,
sweet dopes.

We are white light without a home.

I throw crowns of seagrass
into the lengthy waves.

*

Into the quiver of a woman's body.
And we cannot hand ourselves back.

Nothing, these telescopes.

A string drawn from my mouth
becomes a brooding gull.

No, it is a violin

playing as our nets pull in.

Instead of Soup for Lunch

Come stand in the rain with me.
Then we'll go in and put on pajamas,
the kind with feet included. We'll

sketch plans for the dioramas
of our eyes. All these afternoons:
so pressed into me your back

becomes my chest. Almost I can
trace your breathing, almost we are
the least apparent nova in the room.

Hale

Just like in the art exhibit today, where everyone takes
　　pictures of paintings to look through alone,

　　　　　it only makes sense if you listen with one eye closed.
　　　　　　　　Wet orange leaves. Windows that won't quite shut.

　　　　　If I had the cash, I'd send you samples of every plastic leg
　　on earth. My friend and I once knew a guy named Cash.

He loved how she moussed her hair. And this wasn't
　　the eighties, it was two weeks ago. She's the one

　　　　　who made out with him until his girlfriend showed up.
　　　　　　　　Maybe that's what we're doing here—speeding up until we glow.

　　　　　Robots on the dance floor, we have tied our horses outside.
　　What gallop, what comes from under the brush.

Sometimes doom appears in sequins. Not to mean
　　it is someone in a dress. I mean doom is covered

　　　　　in shiny purple circles sewn on by hand.
　　　　　　　　You have to look close, for all the parts aren't sharp.

　　　　　My friend steps back over the sea and she pries boards
　　from the house. I hold the nails. Little dangers, sleepy

charms. The rain cannot forget itself this fall.
　　An outbreak of marsupials in the backyard.

　　　　　Birds fall into the garden and decide to stay.
　　　　　　　　Before, there was no before. Meanwhile, time is catching up.

　　　　　Contracts as we approach the speed of light
　　and finally I see. My dog is the color of gold leaves.

The leaves are the color of warm beer and I would
　　like to make my voice a collage of axels and joints.

　　　　　Overturned at the bar and the chair no longer sits.
　　　　　　　　Hey honey I'm enough from the south to say *slow down*.

Exception Ode

How a rock clatters into an empty well.
How a woman looks away until she sees round
                                                    her entire head.

You stand in water and break into a thousand—
or is it only five?—red birds flying into my
                                                    eyes and then out.

Are we cardinal or osprey, bifurcate or bivalve?
Wondering, our cat comes to the window and leaves
                                                    over and again.

Eventually the farm falls down and we are left with cisterns
growling on the city roofs, a world where the letter

L really means *eleven*. Oh, the prayers that are flying!

All day, I listen to the woman next door yell at her son.
My sister wants to know what her own husband
                                                    will die from and when.

Every afternoon a new gown arrives and I put it on
then wash the dog. Winds keep asking
for direction and I cannot keep my hand
                                                    plucking the storm

from the sky. No longer can I predict where the balloonist
will leave the basket or if I will attend the party.
Six steps forward is just that. Sunrise may also occur

                                        when we least expect it.

Sequence in the Specific

Each night I make the ice to keep me through tomorrow.
Great trouble, finding someone to say it never mattered.
Somewhere, someone is so much more me.
Once I said we could be anyone: the woman standing in the river at night.
The man calling to her in the day.
Whatever it is, the matter, whatever is gone.
Please relay again the coordinates of a door closing.
Of these increasing tendencies towards violet.
Yes, I took a pine from your yard and planted it in mine.
Yes, I am aware enough of a taste in my mouth, small violets.
Of the man calling to her in the day.
Every word has one day less, even ones stretched between.
The man says and she never turns.
I take the door from your house and attach it to mine on the inside.
An imperfect fit but it keeps those like years out.
This is the part where I am kept on small ice, whatever the tendency.
It's no trouble finding someone. The main calling.
Wherever it is, the matter, wherever is gone.
Then appears a stretch of time running between.
And later, your finger at the corner of the frame.
Everyone has one day less, even rivers at night. The woman.
And here is a girl with ice cupped in her hands.
And here are pines, dying in summer.
A finger at the edge of the wheel.

*

A Positive

After two months the cat
has much to say. A dry
wind moves in.

Messages aren't glass, what is
wrong with your hand?

It falls over my eyes, night
running through broken

branches on our lawn.

Many stars on the ground.
I can't stop touching my
face or talking into cabinets.

Into the bells. Driving
home each night, I ask it *where*.

Fall crickets sing under the air.
I have forgotten how to be
nervous. Now I feed

the cat by hand. I try

to make the wind do something.

Pirouette, I say.
Flambé, I say.

*

This date is not working out,
I call from my side
of a hospital bed.

For years I have said everything
is a rose, decreased.

A stray dog fighting to get
through the door.

Finally I kick it
away, into dry leaves
running up the drive.

Gate closed and anchor up
I pour wine over the bed.
The cat looks on, tumbling

rocks. Every minute is an
idiot lacing his shoes

backwards. Glancing up
to tell me there are more

strings in the drawer.

*

But there is a secret I want
to tell you: my face is the heart

beat of a bird.
We are dancing in

abandoned consistency.
Come and talk under my

ear. Tell the neighbors

to go back to sleep.

The cat and I run
faster through the corn

until we both begin to see
the same spirit in different

bodies. One tells me
I have pretty feet. Very
generous, that guy.

Then he says: *So, do I
get a hug?*

*

How to say: *I am of red fire*
without sounding cousin

to the devil? There is

a secret I want to tell you.
The dog's call lost in the trees.

Lost to what's left. I scoop
up the dirt and whisper.

I come home until
the cabinets are empty.

Come home and leaves
litter the steps.

Yes, that's me running
with a net under each
arm. Thinking of a million

ways to pull in the sky.

Practice Test

My days are made of long data.
Until one night is every night

I am a labman in thick gloves,
I am the woman taking her time.

There are flames to fix, other quite
rights to indulge. In the morning

it was only me stumbling off
with myself, only my mouth

becoming the night sky. We are all
issued white coats. We are forever

taking samples of this world.
I have begun eating breakfast.

I am working on a collection
of orphan tattoos. Toast burns,

rivers break. My days are made
of long data. Anatomical models

walk off and a solitary dissection
ensues. This is the funny part,

where all my clothes are clean.
Surely there's a formula for doubt,

an equation for walking out and into.
No duplicates, just a brief flick

of our wrists until will is contained
by autoclave, by torsion, by rain.

Searching for Calvin Coolidge

Calvin Coolidge and I sit on a leather couch drinking haywire.
There is nothing left to do but look for someone we don't know.

Whistles of creation are sounding and it is *birdie birdie birdie* to the lips
and hair. Calvin Coolidge is an advent calendar. He is scenes behind

twenty-five closed doors. We are vaulting past the mongoose, we are
a confit of speed. Oh Calvin, what we're required to forget might not

be much. With radio voices we sing the color of our eyes. We are over
fog, we are branches jutting through water. I tell Calvin Coolidge

of a bridge named for him and he says *peacock*. He does not darn socks,
Calvin does not have a good stone to his name. We digest the crucible.

We giggle, watching a turkey drive the car. The papers say it is time
for a relapse and we agree, our sweaters are too itchy. So we discard them

in chimneys and leave a little smoldering on the walk. Calvin Coolidge lies
down with dogs and we do nothing about light crashing back through

the world. We pull apples apart and pinch out their wispy blue flames.
We jostle all the babies and put them gentle down to bed. What do I keep

in my mouth amid the blinking goddess, all thrown back? Is it a bright
whip, is it where cantilevers burst forth in blue dress? Our necks tilt

like light fading. Calvin Coolidge and I sit on pillows made of waves and
watch the gamble alight on thin wire. Will he tell me his name again, will he

tie a feather to this hook? Our power is to carry people to places we seek.
Baskets in hand, we are starting off. Oh Calvin we are going this way.

Mountaineer

Once I saw a comet while the world held fast.
Morning in bed, four pennies for my trouble,

unwashed glasses and a bottle: all unmoved.
Give me the margins, give me a brain grown

bored. Workmen at the neighbor's drink
at noon and spit into the street. I bring

my ear down to the yard's level, humming
to the grand exaggeration of being. I can

smooth all lines in the dirt. Roots gently
turn to glass: no volcanoes, no fires. It is easy

to say a world is in motion but difficult to hear
what this means. There are small windows in soil.

Now I am a thousand years ago. I am whatever else
you might say. Tonight the world will hold

fast to the hem of my skirt in the grass, to the moon
giving all its graces away. Nothing the mocking-

birds say makes sense, except that everything
makes sense. Once I was a swirl of bats

over an evening river. I leaned from a bridge
to see my shadow cast in water. No fires,

no volcanoes. Peonies for my troubles still
grow overboard, while planets turn to glass.

The Red Meat Version

And where do you keep your keep?
And where do you store your brushes?
Detritus must be led gently away.
Must be massaged off the bone.
I grow tiny curved claws in which I grasp
The bone-burnished gleam of a rib.
Rib is second fiddle. Rib is keeping time.
We all grow in a swirl, making true

Symmetry rare. Nothing fearful, imperfect
Persistence remaining dear. Rib
Cutting the path of my arms or framing
An embrace. Tiny brush, we scour out.
Think of other ways you are touched.
Which of—when any of—will do?

Three

So I move into a house that smells
like sycamore. So I avoid the place

we bought one spring, three streets
down. In the windows I string star

lights that drift from yellow to green
to red. You are back with the gymnast,

but that doesn't mean days are vaulting
much. It means no one walks the dog

these mornings. It means no one knows
how hard you kiss me when you come

to bring him home. This night I see
we are wedded to an impossible tribe

when I hear Atticus say about Tom:
Last thing I told him was not to lose heart.

Flash Test

The day we drive to the courthouse, two prisoners
      escape from the jail downstairs. You say this is surely

              a good sign; I say they are the state's budget-cut
                  version of doves. Maybe it is our former selves

              bursting from the seams. Thread or scene, how many
  insects can we categorize? Ladybug on synthesizer,

mosquito on bass? We have no air resistance. Our judge sways
      as he reads. I model a thousand millipede dresses. There's a beach

              here under bills, the calls from the clinic, under
                  a couch smelling of our dog. We met and for a year

              didn't speak. For a year I barely thought, just jumped
  on the highway and kept moving. Skated drunk

over a frozen pond in worn sneakers; commuted from Jersey
      into the World Trade Center site. Once I wrote a poem

              about sitting on that train at 6am, how it rocked along.
                  A boring poem, but we weren't supposed to see sunlight

              that far down. This time I'm hoping I am really made out of ants.
  This time we're looking at the phone and saying, *Baby*,

come on. What parts to leave in focus, what bits to leave
      blurred and breathless? Everyone stares into their bathroom

              mirrors, trying to figure out what they think. I offer up
                  my eyebrows, some suspicious freckles, a giant pink

              bottle of shampoo. When guests come over, you leave vials out.
  But I hide mine in the spice drawer, hoping they might become

exquisite and worth much desert travel. Maybe right now you wish
  I would say *breast*. Although I'd like this shirt a little

              lower-cut, I've been living with breasts for a long
                  time. And they are starting to crawl! The ants are up!

This isn't scary, it's a miraculous convolution of stripes, the tumble of time. It's the way I say *run* as I press the shutter down.

Senator of Gravity

Moves, and we devise two marketable affairs.
Insists, and I tear my picture from the Greatest

Flings Calendar. A renewed version, I line
my pants with sequins. I patch the holes

with mysteries of electorates sprung in dirt.
Hungry, we buy the ugliest crown roast.

Suspicious, we keep watch on it for several
weeks. My will is torn to shreds by distant

storms. This Senator and I stare into the same
jurisprudence; share a tattered bootleg of scotch.

I tie the Senator's heart in scarlet yarn. Always
ocular, he insists moss where my eyes should be.

Singing, I paint a cover over the calenture
of finite weather. Bravely, the Senator

locates the last kingdom I'm searching for.
Brings it into our bed of pomegranate and fire.

For the Love of Foucault

Waiting in breath we try to catch the heavy pendulum
while earth and touch play out in meteor and design:

fierce candles burning under snow. A flock of wax-
wings; the web between thumb and finger starting to fail.

Time makes love with abandon but is not kept there.
Mattress is propulsion and vapor, is hidden clockings.

The pendulum holds its path while we continue to lilt:
red dot of stone in your ear, drop of honey in my eye.

After Our Mothers Return to the Armories

Battalions emptied, I stare at a thistle five times
trying to construct a knot in its voice.
I read Chekhov; he mentions women at a distance.

Thunder, and the dog climbs into the bath.
Porch light, and I am the moth tangled in my hair.
I held a woman's hand while she died.

Another coiled and spit on my sleeve.
I stare at a thistle until it is five
wounded bodies galloping to everywhere:

past shipwrecks, past flannel, past the intention
of owls. None of us someone, somewhere
else. Two mosquitoes embrace and fly

a world into a world that is knotted and exact.
Signals relax into the state of sleeping dogs. No
fossils, no oxcarts. Not the inventions of owe.

Goodnight Moon

Say I wake and our house is one million
grey rabbits. Say I dial the numbers and you

won't answer. Say I am tossed among bed
clothes, am lost to solar storms and yellow

paint spilling from a lamp. So what? Then
what? Years ago I wanted a series of parallel

lives, to see how it turns out for all of me:
for self as astronaut or self as raccoon.

For the self as mustachioed or meek.
Today someone asks how I am and I say

Everything. Steady won't keep me from
thinking of the girl in the graveyard,

of the sweet boy drunk outside the gate. Say
I call from the next room and you don't call

back. What then? Say asleep I can feel you
walking towards me; say I am more than what

we thought. Say I call twice and the young girl
in the graveyard is the only one who answers.

So what? Our house is now sleeping rabbits,
walls in a jumble and yellow on my hands.

Everyone Knew it was Roethke

That white camisole I wore to New York one carousel day
is finally starting to wear thin. Maybe I should fold it away

with a couple leaving the scene. Away with the greenhouse
shushing its plants. Of course I don't know, having left

your book under childhood. Of course I don't know, having
given the facts to the shape of the fire.
                                    Oh, Roethke!

We break the horses from the poles; we make love until
all museums close. What happens, what does not. Oh

Roethke, your wife downstairs, we kiss and already
I know that some summers the crepe myrtles blossom

in slow firework; that rainstorms can leave us blinded on
the road. Of course I cannot recite every myth of creation

sprung from the loam, but this doesn't worry you
as I button your vest. As I steal your linen jacket.

What happened is what is not. Have we ever met? Yes,
I know love can sit uneasily in the body. That words

run towards us and we dodge.
                            We kiss, and all the fierce

while I know what everyone knows: people drift off

                            and grow into lilies.

Cunt Diablo, Cock Diane

We listen to our arms rise in the night
To the lullabies of shrimp and steak.
Conflate my surprise, lick the flint—

But only with a sandpaper tongue.
A legion of main courses becomes
Anatomical, so have the curve of me

Open in your teeth. Who is diablo,
Who is diane? For all inventive
Purposes am I wooed and laughing.

The Goddess Resigns

I am seven shattered ficus.
Of few friends, opening towards.
Once headed a household
of beauty, now husbander of turtles.
Desirous of thick socks,
I distribute spent zeros
and look for a place to expand.
I do not keep very still.
I am the samurai who wants you always.
In the months since I made out
like a bandit, my vocabulary
still avoids me. On the tailor's stand
I dodge the pins in my knees.
I break those swans apart.
A kingdom of transit maps
awaits my launch, hems watertight.
Am I fetching? Am I fixative?
Do I have durable teeth?

Of Measures Imperfect and Precise

When I say *roses*, I mean how
to change a light bulb with my teeth. How to peer

through a million wires until I see your fading skin.
I mean understanding when they call the nun

it is best to duck first and then pray along out of
dizziness. She won't find a way to leave the room

fast enough, but at least she will pretend the door
locks. I mean every time I look up, someone

else is staring in. You are here and there. The air
balks then effervesces. Pause and propulsion is all

a matter of balance. When I say *nun*, I mean small
woman who carries the untamed around her body

and I mean the planet of this will heal and I mean
oh darling that I meet every eye looking in.

Colonization

for Chris

Day begins as I issue myself a ticket for mishandling dreams in lit windows.
A large meteor fell and I stood still and it hit me and burst.
My friend is driving to Pennsylvania, she says the roads are wider going east.
That movement can take the role of object desired.
I picked a yellow flower but I was lying.
There is a man who sits in a car, smoking and watching a lit window.
It is all over in a twenty-minute dinner.
In tiny meteors that I stood still for until they burst.
If you are frightened, I'll gather all the wings and take them outside.
I lie to a man, I tell him tinfoil is the perfect size for this idea.
And aphids get the better deal, ants cleaning up the yellow.
My friend is surviving through disdain; I forget to keep watch on the rocks.
On the arena of brief and thin-limbed cranes.
But just once a year, and just enough to remember the way her hand looked.
My friend put her dog to sleep and our other friend cried in her car for an hour.
The rocks lapse while she takes a mile walk inside.
Morning glories twist above a trellis and ants follow.
I want to call my friend and tell her this, but she is driving through five states.
Afternoon and a girl is asleep on a deck, beside a bag of cherries the jays are watching.
I lied to a man, I told him words kept in jars to tell men.
Day ends in a song of antennae and twenty-minute clouds.
About this, about the dog dying, about the objection desired:
I cannot keep my eye on the rocks and they lapse into the first time yes.
We want to pursue the object of what we desire, watching east and wilder.
To find a meteor in Pennsylvania and hide it in the car.

Apparitional

All summer I return to the swimmer.
My feet placed to the edge, I listen

to how he moves with water.
Heart drawn, no other lines.

He mouths words I read. He stays
above level. We have met, I think.

We have met in backstroke, in line,
perhaps in error. Months run

seismic while the static hurtles.
Maybe we are an exhibit of bone

and coin. Of copper and porous
meeting along a wayward spine.

A Perpetuall Light

Sun dives through a window and over
        my feet. We come to the coast, water moving

so we can stay still. My mind spends much time
        explaining to our bodies about the common-

sense of change. You sleep beside me. I have
        a discussion with a skylight about the purpose

of being and then not. Sky says nothing so
        I save my faith for science—for isn't gravity

the best proof of angels? Like everything, an ocean
        must sit and watch while no second on earth

is the same. Maybe one ant slightly alters direction.
        Or laughter dies down and then swells again.

Un, deux, trois, quatre, cinq, six! and cease
        and the sandwich is burnt and we start anew.

In between thoughts I count your breaths. Next
        I try not to count your breaths. How particulate

our lives; how bright the intersections.
        Angels are made of sea salt. Are made of misguided

electricity carving out the wayward sonnet
        of our hearts. Summer fog in the dunes

is such a miracle that I want to reach and take mouthfuls
        from heavy leaves hanging green at the window.

Our old dog presses her sore hip to the floor
        and the young cat cannot stop his purring.

The Art of James Franco

You come home. Long day,
dancing with neon animals.

They have a secret language
which they use to discuss

pixilated flashes sent out
to mimic movement.

Franco, you're excluded

with existence. When you talk
to your wife, she hands you
a baked potato and a shovel.

It is late and you must dig.

*

Your light, the potato glows
and points out where to start.

Digging back among facets
until you are naked and unaware
of what this means. You are

in front of an aggressive English
man. Your wife feeds babies

cooks meat shouts through the
window to *keep going*.

This interested man sprung
from you know not where
takes your cock but you are

tired from the neon animals,
the potato making a face.
You remember

a story of women sewing stripes
on tigers and begin to speak.

Someone whistles and you
think *marmot*.

*

How now, Mr. Franco?
What, ho! How does it feel?

Birds are attached to the sky
and I drive faster. This facet,

you're slumped in the seat,
staring where pavement
meets water. I won't stop

pointing out trees in Portland.
All those potatoes in the trunk,
we never get them to the border

in time. Will the cop believe me
when I say I have never
been so drunk?

*

Naked and not liking it.
Here, facet,

I hand you another drink.
I am wings made of rib bones.

Some of the neon animals come
into the club for a dance.

You've had one of those
but I hear strippers find you
annoying because you are

melting and illuminated ice.

Anyway, the Englishman doesn't
have time for this. He has

to get to Texas.

*

You hold the potato higher
until you can see my eyes

in the boxwoods. Are you looking
at me as you swing the shovel
down? I dance with you

in the third facet, and sometimes
we sit together in the first.
For several years I have tried

to knit this scarf so you can
forget it in a cab on Broadway.

*

Eventually, we run into a wall of
cricket cricket cricket.

I slide under the table at the bar.
I grind the neon animals down.

Your wife's voice swims in glass.
A door opens or closes,
depending on which side you're on.

The Englishman loosened says
Where are you, James Franco,

all faceted in? By the door, leaning
on your shovel. You smile

and raise the precious and long-
standing potato.

Backwards Dynasty

I cannot put a frame down. In history
my arms accumulate all manner

of mail and plate. Swabs of my feet
grow red buttons in agar. Like you, I roll

the garbage to the curb. We may kiss
again, but I will not pick at the body

until I find a place where lineage
finally crossed with rain. The car

backs down the drive. I enjoy a man's
shoulder in the mirror, the brilliance

of the arm entering the body.
Descent is thin in cities, though barns

lose the power to captivate. Recall,
I am not the best judge. Standing taller

into my hat, it covers more of my face
but I can see a blue feather briefly

becoming the painting of a brutal horse.
It seems I fall forever, swallows diving

faster. It's a script when recited: *Good
morning! Are you ok?* Am I about to

apologize. Nothing in anatomy braves
the lower rings of the pelvis. As for me,

I descend in wildflowers and tigers.

*

My Other Life is a Citroën

Filling the car with gas, briefly I
regain a minimal understanding
of how I must rocket out then

spin back to you. This will make
sense sooner if I smoke.
If I can drive for miles with one

arm bent out the window. Surely
my sister never is filled by such
lust for the smell of gasoline.

For places where one is unturned.
Tonight you are home with friends
and I have a carful of groceries.

Everything I could hand to a man
on an underpass corner with his card-
board sign. This will make sense

sooner if the orange cat will stop
waiting out the rain on our porch.
If I did not have to stop myself

from falling into your arms each
day. My own joints and springs are
ready to go, are reading back

issues of the French Revolution.
Shelves full I try to find the cat
as your friends go brightly home

after breaking one wing from
a wooden horse. Still roaring
by our house is the highway.

I hide in back rooms, several
blankets over my head. Our own
oiled cat curls into my lap and so

there is no way to hunt through
dear dark rain for another who
is not mine and passing through.

Little Company

for Sarah

Some hours I pass against, waiting for dark
to rearrange itself, to crowd back and give

two hands to the blade.

One that might excise constellations
or say about the last ship, that long wagon
bearing me forward. Maybe it was

the brief exhalation of my skin

that did us in: letters of your words came
to elide like mortar, pages dim under the ripple

of an orange-water moon.

You said there has to be a vein,

blood mineable. But two lines of brambles

do not make a crown, in this spring where even
the wisteria seems to know the score.

Scattered April lightning and someone calls
to say *tornado*. But in the morning all I see
is weeping cherry and water on the cars,

and the sky which has cleaned itself out.

Mercurial in Retrograde

You were born and knew no one.
The world rendered you converted
and small in the light of her continent-

gown. There were days when nothing
was said better; there were small fires
and you grew larger in pointing.

Someone said you expected too much.
Doubt became febrile voices in retreat.
There was no way to keep up

with the body and its coming to.
You remember three herons, dead;
remember a splinter of marble,

convinced it could be drawn upright.
A frog sits on your head until you cease
imagining its absence. For proof

you would devour a new class of ant.
You would tie stilts to your arms, because
you are tall enough and want everyone

to see you waving without mistake.
Someone says you don't expect enough.
But you are talking to no one. You are

humming into this flock of grackles.

When I Say **Ahoy!**

I mean we are temporarily re-coagulating, loved
one. I mean I drink as many dragonflies as I can.

For a very long time, I have waited to tell you
that the imagination is 5 hounds
                                                    on 100 trails.

That there is only so much that can happen
before your actual eyes, like in the dream where

I'm kissing myself again because it seems
easier than asking the desk clerk if anyone

returned my green cashmere sweater.

At one time it was my job to be beautiful
but now I am here to hand over whatever

else a person can take from the sky. When I say
imagination, I mean driving our dog for x-rays.

I mean taking a sip of wine and kissing
                                        the air around your mouth.

Translated from the Russian

One notices without fidelity
how moss covets stone

and ice crystals build
themselves into cold dirt.

Existence repays the favor
and it becomes easier to love

parenthetically, without ever
mentioning the breasts.

Instead, one is thinking
of people in cafes. One is

attempting to pinpoint creation
in the way keys disappear.

Breakfast in Bed

A girl hides one eye under
Her hair while revising
An agreement to have sex

With a friend and telling me
She loves unicorns. Generally,
I distrust their proximity

To virgins and bored tapestries.
But I wouldn't mind having
A mythical beast to myself.

The Jesus Year

In your dreams, you never escape.
Alligators always secret you away.
When you look in mirrors you're certain
the back of your head is turning
into your mother's. Suddenly
conversation is a white web. Is it
ever just a kiss? You are not one
for gymnastics but the leotard
indicates otherwise. When you wake
you sit in a series of chairs and
try to corner perspective.
Meanwhile, sleep takes stock.
In daylight someone points you
toward rocket science, but cannot
name the bones of the feet.
You wanted rest and were allowed.
You could not conceive it differently.
Eventually stars become another version
of what happened when you looked away.

Young Love

Oh red umbrellas thrust into the sun! A drunk sings
to nets of tulle in an ocean, to whales who forget how it feels
to barrel through salmon. Sunrise turns everything into something
else. I push the mass of myself against an idea of sunset.
This turns my feet into wicking flames.
Reaching upward is suppressed. Casting down is suppressed.
Whitman changes two words but I forget whose,
even without odd corners and tables under which to lose a drunk.
Caught in a stare upon this cup, I overlook what runs to and from it:
a boy at the counter with a birthmark on his neck.
In spilled sugar I write: *My feet are wicking flames* but you are looking
at the girl who runs her hand along the boy's back.
I think there are songs about the limitation of a body to not change:
So Egg Until Pickle. Then Egret Until Hamster on Wheel.
Shifted words are a man in a yellow hat, weaving down a road.
Regrets! sing the chairs. Upend me! shout the clouds.

Two

Twilight and two women walk by. I hear as
they pass *we won't put catastrophe in our bodies.*

Leaves fell from the maple in the backyard
as we talked this afternoon, as I put my palm

against the cool white of the sink. What
can be denied when the sky is oil and crayon?

When I was twenty-seven I sat with dying
strangers. Ten years later I am a dog with six

legs. I am the far woman on the phone singing
all the songs I can: the ballad of tears in aspic.

An opera by a flock of three-eyed gulls.

Call Me

Hello, baby! I'm flicking slivered almonds off the top
of this croissant, aiming straight at the birds. Hello

baby, I am David Byrne and the almonds are wishing
I might stop this singing. But last night your phone rang.

When someone you are in love with is called at 2am,
sleep is powdered milk, and you should consider

planting more turnips in the garden. They are the most
rooted vegetable and you need to learn to dig in.

When I'm David Byrne and upset, I sit in the bathroom,
close my eyes, snap my fingers and hum until I forget how

to speak. Until a sundial reflects on the inside of my eyelids
and radishes dance along my spine. No one loves everyone,

is what the fortune cookie should say. No one loves every
one, the days of the week mutter to themselves. Hello

baby! I'm pouring ten packets of sugar into a coffee.
I'm counting on the end of the week and coming up bound.

Even being David Byrne is just an approximation, a little
number I slip into so as to distract my thoughts from last

night when the air suddenly spun into sand, rabbits all
hiding away. Don't worry, baby. I only read the letters

as David Byrne, and he doesn't even know your name.
He doesn't believe a spade and monogamy will make me

a gardener, a faulty comet, or a sun that never wants to set.
Thank God for the little sparrows hopping after my crumbs.

Really Going Places

Another three nights deep in bed and spent
reading through biographies of distant stars.
They shift quietly above a red net of gauze

unrolled across the sky each night. As I twirl
with bread in mouth, with coffee in hand.
A clutch of little armors when the curtains slip

down. Aren't we all lost each night, as stars turn
to others, signals strong or faint? How I look
out this window does not transfer. It just simply

disappears. Three nights become five and still
deep the pages begin to wear down. Six and all
I have is a basket of moonlight, rolled into blue

pearls. Tomorrow I must plan to throw hooks
into the sun and pull down a few tendrils of light.
Braid them into my hair then softly dry my face.

Boat in the Harbor of My Own Particulars

Anchors far from the floating dock.
Is brimming with my missing sandal's
history. Is covered with a blue blanket
before my sister and I slice it apart.
She throws a green ball; it waits
unsteady until a dog swims out.
The keel secrets two dresses, only.
Every shoreline blinks a distant spell.

Tonight the water breaks a moon
over its waves. We polish one oar,
push it deep between bracken currents
and their gradient of starlight.
We sink in, air now pocked in the cliffs.
In the bow I wind my oiled hair tightly.

The Bride, Unbuttoned

for Layla

Getting older is like walking up the stairs backwards.
  Or so I tell two girls at a party where I meet

        a man who will sit too close to me next week.
            Those young women simmer in skirts

        and white boots. White boots are difficult to carry off,
  especially in Maine's rainy season. I offer them water

but it's the wrong color. All my sentences return, unopened.
  As though recording this all has ever been a choice, I wish

        I could wear less clothing—but I get cold in the summer.
            I am picking up my half of a bargain, dusting it off

        with an orange sequined skirt. Maybe I don't just want a girl
  to fool around with, macaroni or not—someone with this number

called me three times today. Later I hear the man drove
  off through plate glass air, through a series of three nudes,

        wrecking it for everyone. Don't try and see up the stairs
            or you'll scare the shit out of yourself. That is all

        I can come up with. In Manhattan may there be farms
  that grow upwards. May I continue in attraction to linear man,

to female motion under cotton. Worlds move all around, worlds spin past.
  Flashbulbs for eyes, brushstroke for mouth, I just stand here.

        My mug says *Teri*. My mug says *Sea World of Texas*. I think Teri is more
            likely, though I can't reach her to confirm. Being scared

        is generally a good sign: you're about to learn something
  about the way dinner tastes when bears are running up and down

the stairs. Keep eating, chew thoroughly, don't choke. I'm really getting
  to like you. Let's draw a castle on aluminum and watch it wick away.

Hangman's Guide to Love

Kept away from the party, bustled off from flame, I work in the world's
smallest room. Detached, oh love, detached, I have forgotten the five
names I once knew. Every day a friend calls and repeats their order.

Every morning I open an orange, my closest experience to elemental lust.
But love it is no use: boxes arrive and again my dog licks herself lame.
A man sits on your bed, smokes a cigarette, and you wonder what you wanted.

But how gentle a cloud's stupidity—what balm against an accurate break.
The wider the eyes, the further I fall in: hurricanes, babies, twenty-five-
year-old girls. Lakes, if I can rise high enough to pause and peer down.

Prometheus Day

What is found in the ventriloquist's neurons

or lost in the barrel of the shotgun.

An existential kiss envelops which
parts of the night sky.

Which floodings.

*

List the reasons a woman has
for washing her face.

Watch the fog sit thick in the trees.

From the plane, ground lights flow like lava.
From her window, deer in twilight.

Here, again: the way we watched the mountain
from your porch.

The way it was still there when we woke

*

into the fate of two dogs walked at dusk.
Of a cat behind a window.

The manner in which I wake into,
like a child shouting *Stick!*

Into how I once said nothing with my touch.

Is it sparks of light ice, skin garnering green.

*

Or is it wood smoke, thickening the trees.
What is outside that which envelops?

Finding the night is made of cloth ties.
Finding the sort of stone only a lover can.

Resetting the mountains
in proportion to the sky.

Upon the Advice to be a Bad Girl

What is the opposite of tornado?
Red stars in the crook of elbows
or a penny in my basket of tales?
I move my knee closer to ignition.
At the store I buy shipwrecks and cock
crows. I buy laces and wood ducks.
I fall into the way you clasp your hands.
Meanwhile, my friends are out drinking.
My friends are dancing on folded floors.
I shorten the distance between us.
Who can address the social disaster
of crickets in the field at dawn?
So I followed you back from the river,
a beer in each hand. So I filmed
vertebrae running to fuse. Brought
us into the cellar, to the chickens
caught in a wind above provision.

Twenty Minutes in New Canaan

To a southern ear, *New Canaan* sounds nearly like *New Haven*.
Caught in this direction I photograph a pigeon, pink clouds, a man.

> A flock of birds rises from oaks and becomes elastic in air—
> halved and halved, pieces break off and head to different horizons.

A phone rings and I feel there is something specific you would like to say
about the pigeon, or about the man trying to put his arm around

> a girl. About the inky silhouettes of those birds. About the way you
> put your lips to a cup as we wait on this platform. Once

you said *anadromous* means we are born inland and swim to the sea.
Each night one fall we cracked windows along the river's bank,

> the sound of moonlight on water part of a myth we chased. But waiting
> knows little of wind; knows less of salt. I am sleepy and I bite my nails.

Whether we are safe or biblical, I don't care. Is there something you intend
to say, about you and me missing the train? If everything is one thing

> then the woman on the phone is the cup in your hands. Is the light
> on the film in its frame. The pigeon, walking off. Why do salmon turn

saltwise as they knock against the sea? I ask. Maybe love, you say.
Maybe, I say, pointing upwards. Now look what the sky is flying back.

Finally, My Neighbor Borrows an Egg

You could say *My brain has a mind of its own*
and everyone would sigh and fall asleep.
I would mention my interest in your mouth

but that doesn't seem very electric.
We might talk more about fog, but that
isn't an appropriate subject during lunch.

I've forgotten the point of Ecclesiastes.
Of trees trying to shake themselves free.
It was just one egg. I've been asleep for days.

One

Kiss wet paint and you'll leave
a mark. Lacking a better idea

we planned our wedding five
times. Two or three trophies

attended; the duchess ran off
with the magician. It's always

this way, the Buddhists tell me.
A bear sings in the backyard.

Little Birds

In California my bachelor wears a flouncy
little skirt until he is equine until he is objet

d'art: a small worn Chagall in my pocket.

Aloud I read Nin's soft porn.
Her words fall into the shape of an ear.

Where are all the children I've left behind?
Where is the plague of sitars?

Oh, I am a failed smoker but a fine boot maker.

Too late so off to sleep I read to him aloud
my mouth half in wine half in

the rattle of trolley cars dim in the fog.

I am a bad girl I am a bad boy I am adept
at differentiating between skin and cypress.

Until the ear falls away and I can pocket sound.
Until the cock of a finger, the wink of an eye:

gotcha buddy let's see what's under that skirt.

*

We are ink in a hotel bed, we are breath
across questionable sheets.

I dream these walls of azure feathers;
of flame green unshelling in my hand.

The hotel window opens four
inches and I whisper dirty Nin to the cold.

Asleep he misses the swing of my hips.
But he used to live close by, and nearby

misses nothing. Now I am a blue
horse, now a solitary violin playing

along the hill. He leaves the skirt on
and I don't bother.

I rub Nin on my face
until the fog howls.

*

It's not the donkey in the bath
but the water washing out the tub.

From the other room, the bachelor
he moans in the skirt.

I turn on a variety of lamps
but never take a picture.

I jump on the bed and he snores harder.
I text dirty messages to girls he'd like to fuck

among these ghosts: ten or so heartfelt
medications, a tiger who fancies

herself the subject of Lucian Freud.
Why did the small girl go walking

through the desert scrub?
Why do the dying fall in love with the dying?

What else is there to do.

*

Nin's ear follows us to the beach.
Anemones, anchored stars & soft as

a cat paw. Stripped I sit in the tidal pool,
unlit until small fish swim my length

and I can see his face above the incoming.
Believe me static; believe me a pier.

Adhere, adhere line of girls, dust of fog,
missing children in deserts and swells.

Nin is on my foot. His skirt is on the sand.
Where am I jumping where do I pounce?

The object surprised by its artist:
I will hammer those heels on tight.

What gathers on each side of the waves.
Two of my fingertips are birds in pale flight.

When we are gone we are everywhere
and I kiss a hoof of the horse beside me.

NOTES

The epigraph is from H. L. Hix's sonnet sequence, "The God of Window Screens and Honeysuckle" (sonnet 40; *Shadows of Houses*, Etruscan Press, 2005).

p. 9: "The Name of the World" was written in response to the line "Tell me the name of the world" in Robert Penn Warren's poem, "Audubon: A Vision," (*Selected Poems of Robert Penn Warren*, LSU Press, 2001).

p. 49: Anton Chekhov writes of "women at a distance" in his story, "The Kiss."

p. 50: The title is taken from the children's book *Goodnight Moon* by Margaret Wise Brown.

p. 51: "The shape of the fire" is the title of a poem by Theodore Roethke.

p. 56: "Apparitional" refers both to Bill Lundberg's film installation, "Swimmer," and to the exhibit "Mission/Missions (How to build a Cathedral)" by Cildo Meireles.

p. 57: The phrase "a perpetuall light" is found in the papers of 17th century chemist Robert Boyle.

p. 78: The title and poem are influenced by Marcel Duchamp's "The Large Glass."

ACKNOWLEDGMENTS

Deepest gratitude to the editors of *Bat City Review*, *Big Bell*, *Borderlands*, *Crazyhorse*, *Denver Quarterly*, *Forklift*, *OH*, *Mississippi Review*, and *Narrative Magazine* for giving several of these poems their first homes.

Heartfelt appreciation to Debra Allbery, Layla Barker Billings, Elyse Fenton, Laurie Filipelli, Lynn Francis, Henry Kearney, Maurice Manning, J. Mickela Sonola, Dara Wier, Alan Williamson and Dean Young, and to the communities of writers at Warren Wilson College and UMASS Amherst, all for their invaluable encouragement and support, and for reading this manuscript in its various forms along the way.

I would like to extend special thanks also to *The Pedestal Magazine*, *Tar River Poetry*, the North Carolina Arts Council, the Poet Fools, the Bear Rock Poets, the Community of Writers at Squaw Valley, and my family.

And infinite love to Nate Pritts and the H_NGM_N BKS editorial board, and to Scott O'Connor for the cover design, to Nate Slawson for the book design, and to Liubomir Turcanu for the cover photograph.

Laurie Saurborn Young is a poet, writer and photographer, and has worked in factories, in the mental health field, and with hospice organizations. She holds an MFA from the low-residency program for writers at Warren Wilson College, and has studied in the Program for Poets and Writers at the University of Massachusetts, Amherst. Her photographs have been exhibited in Austin, Texas, and Southampton, New York. *Paul's Window II*, her photograph of the NYC skyline, appeared on the cover of the book *Fall Higher*. She lives in Austin, Texas.